The Department of Soul Reclamation

by Courtney Kessler-Jeffrey

Mneme Press
http://mnemepress.org

The characters and events in this book are fictitious. Any similarity to real persons, living or dead, is coincidental and not intended by the author.

Book design by Rebecca A. Demarest

The fonts in this book include:
Dream Orphans by Typodermic Fonts and
Athelas by TypeTogether

Printed in the United States of America by *kdp.com*

The Department of Soul Reclamation

For Performance Rights

Please contact Courtney Kessler-Jeffrey
at court.kessler@gmail.com

Characters

THE GHOST OF CHRISTMAS PAST: Female-identifying, any adult age, person of colour. The veteran - talented, competent, and bitter; "glaring" could easily be listed among her special skills. Her work is legendary, but she carries some heavy baggage.

THE GHOST OF CHRISTMAS PRESENT: Any gender identity, any young adult age, any race. The newbie - enthusiastic, bright-eyed & bushy-tailed. Goes through every phase of life throughout the course of the play.

THE GHOST OF CHRISTMAS FUTURE: Male-identifying, any adult age, any race. The recently promoted - Clever and playful, his brilliance and skill are frequently overshadowed by those around him. He has a lot of great, forward-thinking ideas - if only he could get someone to take him seriously.

EBENEZER SCROOGE: Male-identifying, 50's to 60's, any race, British accent. The voice is key: this is a recorded role; he is never seen onstage.

It is the playwright's intention for this show to be cast diversely and inclusively. It is strongly encouraged that all races, orientations, genders, abilities, and sizes be considered for these roles.

Setting

Christmas Eve, 1843

The Christmas Office of the Department of Soul Reclamation, a room very much akin to a theatre green room–a couch, chairs, etc. with a smattering of Christmas decor. Three doors off to one side for "dressing rooms," opposite those doors is a door leading to the hallway, and upstage center is a curtain the ghosts pass through for their visits with Scrooge. In the center of the room is a stand, upon which sits a large, ornate bowl of wassail, used to observe the subject and visits.

Stave I

Stave I
Office Hours

AT RISE: PAST *enters from the hallway, fully dressed in white and silver, something practical and amalgamous of bygone eras. She sets down a leather dossier and a thick, official-looking tome. She looks around the room, mentally settling back in. Things have changed. She doesn't like it. She crosses to the wassail, looks in, and consults the dossier. Seemingly satisfied, she exits to her dressing room.*

As she does so, FUTURE *enters from his dressing room, wearing a robe over some state of "I don't want to put my costume on yet" undress and humming (or whistling, or singing) "Last Christmas" by Wham!. He lays out some tinsel. It doesn't go with the decor, but he enjoys it. Checking the wassail, he adds a cinnamon stick to the bowl before exiting.*

As he does so, PAST *pops her head out. She sniffs the air. Something's off. She crosses to the wassail. She removes the extra cinnamon stick (who would put that in there?!) and neurotically adjusts minute details around the bowl before exiting to her dressing room.*

As she does so, FUTURE *enters, still humming rather enthusiastically. He carries one end of an extension cord over to a string of Christmas lights and plugs them in. Their twinkling delights him. Passing the wassail, he drops the cinnamon stick back in as he exits.*

As he does so, PAST *enters from her dressing room, warming up vocally.*

PAST: What a to-do to die today, at a minute or two til two;
a thing distinctly hard to say, but harder still to do.
We'll beat a tattoo, at twenty to two-

> *During her line, she removes the cinnamon stick again.*
> FUTURE *enters, a Trapper Keeper (his dossier on Scrooge)*
> *tucked under his arm. He stops dead in his tracks at the*
> *sight of her. She does not see him immediately.*

PAST: *(cont'd)* -a rat-tat-tat- tat-tat-tat- tat-tat-tat–

FUTURE: Past!?

> PAST *swings around at the sound of his voice.* FUTURE *is*
> *thrilled, if a little surprised, to see her. She is...*

PAST: Future.

> *... less enthusiastic.*

FUTURE: You're back?!

PAST: Aye.

FUTURE: I didn't know–

PAST: Nay?

FUTURE: Where- Why- How've you been?

PAST: Rancorous.

FUTURE: So, not much has changed...

PAST: I was removed from the field.

FUTURE: Yeah, that's what they told me. I'm sorry.

PAST: Relegated to clerical duties these two years. Ne'er has a
soul suffered a heavier burden than that of being chained
to a desk.

4

FUTURE *does a poor job of hiding his amusement at this statement.*

PAST: *(cont'd)* Wherefore do you chortle at my expense?

FUTURE: *(pulling himself together)* Heavy chain. Burden. Awful. Serious. Got it.

PAST: Find it amusing, do you, for this department's highest ranking Spirit to be demoted to such a menial position?

FUTURE: The second highest ranking Spirit in this department feels like this is a trick question...

PAST: Your attempt at humour is noted - and unappreciated.

FUTURE: Don't act like you didn't miss me.

PAST: "Miss" you? I cannot attest to such thoughts.

FUTURE: Okay, rude.

PAST: Hardly.

FUTURE: What are you doing back? No one mentioned anything and I thought you'd be gone longer... Like, a lot longer...

PAST: My supposition was much the same. However, the answer to such a query lies in this.

> *She brandishes her Scrooge dossier, leather-bound with ribbon bookmarks protruding every which way.*

FUTURE: *(noting his own disorganized Trapper Keeper dossier)* Why is yours nicer than mine?

PAST: Future.

FUTURE: Right. You mean our case?

PAST: You have read it?

FUTURE: Duh.

PAST: Then perhaps you have already taken note of this particular subject's, shall we say–

FUTURE: Assholery?

PAST: Your penchant for ridiculous verbiage has not waned, I see.

FUTURE: Why fix what ain't broke?

PAST: But aye, he is quite the... "prick."

FUTURE: *(offering a fist bump)* Nice anachronism!

PAST: *(unsure of what else to do, she awkwardly pats the proffered fist)* Thank you.

FUTURE: We'll work on that. Anyway, yeah, this Scrooge guy - he's the worst! Like, literally the worst.

PAST: Indeed. I have ne'er seen a human more misanthropic.

FUTURE: He'll be a challenge, to say the absolute least, but I think–

PAST: Precisely. A challenge! A challenge hand-selected for me. 'Tis the reason behind my heretofore unforeseen return to the field.

FUTURE: Wait, you think they brought you back for this case specifically?

PAST: Aye! Following last year's antics, 'twas clear to Time and Fate that my absence here was a detriment.

FUTURE: Hey, we did just fine without you, thanks very much.

PAST: Your successful mission last year was due only to your subject becoming so intensely frightened that she turned to God for salvation from the "demons" tormenting her. You inspired fear, not change.

FUTURE: Yeah, but she was still saved! Soul reclaimed. Boom!

PAST: Considering the results, the administration begrudgingly concluded that my skills are better utilized here.

FUTURE: I wish they'd've said something to me, but whatever...

PAST: They could not allow my return to be so elementary, oh no, thus was dredged up the most arduous, futile case they could muster. They mean to make a mockery of me, Future, but I shall instead prove my virtue. I have no intention of moving on or–

FUTURE: Whoa, whoa, whoa - moving on? Past, that's a very serious accusation!

PAST: Calm thyself. I speak only of retirement. Your panic is needless.

FUTURE: Don't do that to me. Word choice is super important!

PAST: Future.

FUTURE: Right. Mockery, challenges, assholes, etcetera... I don't know. That's really low, even for Fate, and she's a salty bitch.

PAST: Convoluted, perhaps, but should I succeed, this could be my chance to break free from that damned desk.

FUTURE: Yay?

PAST: Have you heard? It has been dubbed "The Impossible Job."

FUTURE: Who said that?

PAST: I was informed of this by The Ghost of New Year's Eve.

FUTURE: The "Spirit of Regrettable Snogging?" She's an idiot!

PAST: The administration, the other departments - They all believe me incapable of closing this case.

FUTURE: You can't let those ninnies get to your–

PAST: A betting pool has been opened.

FUTURE: Oh! What's it up to?

PAST: Condescension. How refreshing.

FUTURE: It's part of my charm!

PAST: You exhaust me.

FUTURE: There. That's the peppy Christmas Spirit I know and admire.

PAST: No more of this fooling about. We ought to begin our work.

FUTURE: Oh! Yes! I've actually jotted down some ideas...

> FUTURE *reaches into his dressing room and produces a thick, white plastic binder with multi-coloured tabs. The cover reads: "Future's Super Awesome Plan to Save Scrooge's Soul." It's very clearly more than "some ideas." He's very proud of it.*

PAST: What is that?

FUTURE: My binder. I made a binder.

PAST: Wherefore?

FUTURE: Well, umm, you see, I was under the impression you wouldn't be back, so I, uh, came up with my... own... plan.

PAST: What is the inscription on the front?

FUTURE: "Future's Super Awesome Plan to Save Scrooge's Soul."

PAST: Such... alliteration.

FUTURE: I thought it was catchy. Why? What's your plan called?

PAST: The Plan.

FUTURE: Damn. That's a good title.

PAST: That is a very fine looking tome, Future, but–

FUTURE: Actually...

PAST: Please, allow me to finish my–

FUTURE: I was hoping, well, planning, really, to take on more of a leadership role this year. See, I- I made a binder.

PAST: And I applaud your initiative, 'tis very refreshing, but that will not be necessary.

FUTURE: But... you see, I put a lot of work into this and maybe if you gave it a little peruse, you'd see there's some really good ideas–

PAST: Future, it has been decreed: We must proceed with... this.

> PAST *holds up the large tome she brought in earlier. Embossed in gold on the cover are two words: "The Plan."*

FUTURE: But... that's an office-printed plan. Time and Fate write those... for training purposes...

PAST: I am aware.

FUTURE: But that means- Oh. Oh. They really are–

PAST: 'Tis far from my preference, but we have strict instructions to follow. Deviation is unacceptable.

FUTURE: "We?" Why "we?" I don't see how the rest of us factor into your–

PAST: *(spotting the clock)* The hour grows late. Have we received any word on Present?

FUTURE: *(the change of topic has not gone unnoticed)* None that I've heard.

PAST: 1843 ought to be of age by now.

FUTURE: *(checking The Plan)* According to this, '43 is late.

PAST: Another plotted hindrance, I am certain.

FUTURE: This plan is garbage! You have to see that.

PAST: Who is now the melodramatic one?

FUTURE: It's rigid and impersonal. There's no substance, no spice!

PAST: Spice?

FUTURE: You know, the "spice of life?"

PAST: Do you speak of salt?

FUTURE: Are you messing with me?

PAST: Who is to say...

FUTURE: You hate this, right? You must hate this.

PAST: My feelings regarding the details of The Plan are inconsequential.

FUTURE: My plan is beautiful. I was gonna try this new thing and set aside time for a brainstorming session!

PAST: "Brain... storming?"

FUTURE: You know, incorporate everyone's thoughts and ideas.

PAST: To what purpose? I can see no benefit to–

> *Offstage, a joyous laugh echoes down the hall.*

PRESENT: *(excitedly)* Down this way? Thank you, and Merry Christmas!

PAST: *("Oh God!")* Oh Father Time...

PRESENT: *(singing offstage, getting closer)* "Hark the herald angels sing-"

FUTURE: Past...

PRESENT: *(offstage, closer still)* "-Glory to the newborn King!"

FUTURE: Well, they seem enthusiastic!

PAST: That would not be my word of choice...

PRESENT: *(offstage, just outside the door)* Wow. The Christmas Department! This. Is. Incredible.

PAST: Gird your loins.

FUTURE: Girded.

> PRESENT *bursts excitedly and confidently into the room. Despite their adult size, they are only about 13 or 14 years old mentally. They are dressed simply in a shirt and trousers appropriate to the time period and carry an armload of paperwork and dossiers. A sprig of holly is pinned to their shirt.*

PRESENT: Hello there! Wow! Hi! Good evening!

> PAST *is unenthused.* FUTURE *chuckles.*

PRESENT: *(cont'd)* Merry Christmas!

PAST: You are late.

PRESENT: Well, I'm present now!

FUTURE: Ha! Wordplay.

PRESENT: 1843, reporting for duty! You can call me Present.

PAST: 'Tis your title, is it not?

PRESENT: Wow. You're the Ghost of Christmas Past! I can't believe I'm meeting you! You're a legend!

PAST: Of course I am.

PRESENT: I want to be just like you when I grow up.

PAST: Mmm... that is...

> FUTURE *gives her a "be nice" look*

A kind sentiment...

> FUTURE *shoots her a "Good Job!" thumbs up.*

FUTURE: Present, welcome!

PRESENT: The Ghost of Christmas Yet-to-Come?

FUTURE: Call me Future. Come, join us.

PRESENT: *(sitting down)* I can't believe I get to work with you!

PAST: Your tardiness has set us behind schedule and there is a great deal of work yet to be done. Do not waste your time lollygagging.

PRESENT: No lollygagging here: I brought reading material!

FUTURE: What is all that? "War and Peace?"

PRESENT: Never heard of it.

FUTURE: Longest book ever written? It's, like, a million pages?

PAST: That book does not yet exist.

FUTURE: Really? Dammit.

PRESENT: It may be a lot, but I figured I have all night, so I brought along some reading materials, including a few of your previous case reports to brush up on your style—such page turners! There are some truly miraculous about-faces in here!

FUTURE: Yeah, we've had some good ones over the years.

PRESENT: *(to* PAST, *very seriously)* You're my idol.

FUTURE: Dude, I'm right here.

PRESENT: I feel so lucky to be on your team this year! And working the "Impossible Job," too! I mean, is this real life?

PAST: *(to* FUTURE*)* They are aware that they are a ghost, correct?

PRESENT: What? *(to* FUTURE*)* What does she mean?

FUTURE: She's making unnecessary assumptions about your cognizance. *(quietly, aside)* You do know that we're ghosts, right? Spirits?

PRESENT: *(Is this a trick question?)* Yes?

FUTURE: Okay, cool. Just wanted to double check.

PRESENT: May I ask a question?

FUTURE: Ask away.

PRESENT: You're the Ghost of Christmas Yet-To-Come. Can't you look ahead and tell us how this whole thing is going to go?

FUTURE: Not anymore. See, once Scrooge's case was accepted, his timeline is no longer fixed, so if I look into his future it's all cloudy.

PRESENT: Oh, I see. And the outcome of our work will be reflected in his timeline when we're through?

FUTURE: Yeah, you got it.

PRESENT: And those chains - what becomes of them?

FUTURE: If we succeed–

PAST: Scrooge's chain was wrought by every poor, selfish decision he has made throughout the course of his life. Should we be successful with his case, his decisions from this point forward will henceforth alleviate the weight he bears.

PRESENT: I see, I see. We're a bit like Mister Scrooge's guardian angels, aren't we?

PAST & FUTURE: *(in unison)* Don't compare us to those feathery twats.

PRESENT: I'm so sorry...

PAST: You have been briefed on our subject?

PRESENT: Yes, I have Mister Scrooge's dossier in this stack somewhere...

PAST: You ought to begin acquainting yourself with the Plan–

PRESENT: *(brandishing a period-appropriate copy of* FUTURE'*s plan)* Oh, I've already read it! Got it right here.

PAST: Beg pardon?

PRESENT: *(to* FUTURE*)* I thought you came up with a really interesting approach. The time allotted for us to contribute our own ideas? Brilliant!

FUTURE: At last! Someone who appreciates me.

PAST: We shall not be following the plan crafted by Future.

PRESENT: Oh? Apologies, no one told me.

PAST: *(passing the Plan to* PRESENT*)* We are to adhere to this.

PRESENT: But this is an office-printed plan. Time and Fate write–

PAST & FUTURE: We know.

PRESENT: But why? I thought your plan was quite good.

FUTURE: And I appreciate that more than you'll ever know, but–

PAST: We are to follow the official Plan to the letter. We are under a great deal of scrutiny. Deviation is unacceptable.

PRESENT: I don't get it. Is this a test of some sort?

FUTURE: It's a long story...

PAST: Our time grows short. Let us not waste it.

> PRESENT *begins to dutifully read through The Plan.* FUTURE *checks the clock.*

FUTURE: And who's supposed to be telling Scrooge that he's about to have a very rough night?

PAST: Mr. "I-Cannot-Rest" himself: Jacob bloody Marley.

FUTURE: It's a Marley case? Ugh! That explains everything.

PRESENT: I don't understand.

FUTURE: You see, Marley died- How many years has it been?

PAST: Seven. He died seven years ago this very night.

FUTURE: And every year since, he's gone into the office, shaking his chains like a maniac, begging for us to redeem his horrible friends.

PRESENT: That's admirable!

FUTURE: It's annoying. I mean, like, just because you regret pissing away your Free Will doesn't mean you get to cut in line to get your horrible friends fixed, alright?

PAST: We are not to be faulted for his wretched decisions and wasted time on Earth.

FUTURE: *(to* PAST*)* A Marley case approved... They really are letting you have it, aren't they?

> *A bell chimes.* PAST *crosses to the wassail bowl and looks in.*

PRESENT: Which notice is that?

PAST: Marley has made first contact with Scrooge.

FUTURE: Ugh. Moaning, groaning, or clanking?

PAST: Groaning. As a door knocker. Subtlety is clearly not in that ghost's repertoire.

FUTURE: A door knocker? Who does he think he is–Lewis Carroll?

PRESENT: *(flipping though his dossier)* Who is that? Someone from Mister Scrooge's childhood?

PAST: Lewis Carroll is an eleven year old child. *(to* FUTURE*)* You have gotten ahead of yourself again.

PRESENT: *(yawning)* Gee, I'm sleepy all of the sudden.

FUTURE: Why don't you have a nap?

PRESENT: Oh, I wouldn't want to miss anything!

FUTURE: You won't miss much–

> PRESENT *has dozed off.*

FUTURE: *(cont'd)* Aaaand, down they go.

PAST: They slumber? Future, wake them. We have not the time for–

FUTURE: Give them a break. They're a growing spirit.

Checking the wassail

Wow, Marley's really pushing that chain imagery, isn't he?

PAST: The emphasis is indeed overt, but you recall the usage of the term "impossible," aye? Scrooge is a doubter.

FUTURE: Right... this is gonna be fun.

PAST: Does your definition of "fun" inclu–

> FUTURE *gives her a look.*

PAST: *(cont'd, disdainfully)* Sarcasm.

FUTURE: I know how much you love it.

PAST: I most certainly do no–

> FUTURE *gives her a "Gotcha!" look.*

PAST: *(cont'd)* Oh, damn it all.

> *A clock chimes.* PRESENT *jolts awake. They have aged through their nap and are now 18 or so years in age.*

PRESENT: I'm up! I'm up! Did I miss anything?

FUTURE: *(to* PAST*)* That's a quarter past.

PAST: Thank you quarter past.

> *(returning to her warm-ups)*

A Tudor who tooted a flute
tried to tutor two tooters to toot.
Said the two to their tutor,
"Is it harder to toot?
or to tutor two tooters to toot?"

> *As she finishes her line, she exits to her dressing room.*

FUTURE: You didn't miss much. Marley's visit just wrapped up.

PRESENT: *(opening The Plan)* Better keep reading, then. Say, are there any bites around here? I'm starving.

FUTURE: I knew I should have brought those Christmas cookies! They were shaped like ghosts and everything!

PRESENT: I'll be alright. Do you know why we received this Plan so late? Seems strange considering there was already a Plan in place.

FUTURE: Because Past was brought back at the last minute and this Plan came with her.

PRESENT: Brought back? Has she been away?

FUTURE: You don't- ? Ah, well, like I said, it's a long story.

> FUTURE *peers into the wassail. He takes a whiff of its aroma. It doesn't feel right.*

FUTURE: *(cont'd)* Ugh! Is there no cinnamon in this? How are we supposed to inspire any change with this bland nonsense? *(picking up a cinnamon stick)* Let's spice things up a little bit.

PRESENT: What are you doing? The recipe here doesn't say–

FUTURE: Calm down. It's one cinnamon stick.

> FUTURE *drops the cinnamon stick into the bowl. He waits a moment - nothing. He turns to* PRESENT *and–*

PAST: *(offstage)* What in the name of Father Time himself have you done?!

> PAST *bursts out of her dressing room.*

FUTURE: Past– ?

PAST: Future.

FUTURE: Right.

> PAST *angrily races to the wassail and carefully removes the cinnamon stick.*

PAST: *(turning on* FUTURE*)* What is it you are trying to do?

> *The clock chimes again.*

FUTURE: Half past.

PAST: *(seething with rage)*Thank you half past.

FUTURE: Let's relax–

PAST: Were my words not clear? "To the letter" is a phrase you comprehend, aye?

FUTURE: Come on–

PAST: Any adjustments, however minor, can ruin m- our chances of success. You have just risked–

> *The deep, ominous sound of a bell rings.* PAST *and* FUTURE *swing around to the clock.* PRESENT *is... so confused.*

PAST: Nay!

FUTURE: What is happening? Why?

PRESENT: *(slightly panicked)* What's going on?

PAST: *(calling out to some unseen force)* Please! Nay! 'Twas a mistake! I did not–

> *The Spirits watch in horror as the ominous bell rings 11 more times while the clock rolls forward 24 hours.*

FUTURE: Past, tell me that didn't just happen.

PAST: The plan was to be followed exactly as written! Deviation is unacceptable.

FUTURE: They just took away an entire day's worth of time, Past! A whole damn day!

PRESENT: Oh Father Time...

FUTURE: Did you know this was going to happen?

PAST: This? Nay, not this.

The clock chimes again.

FUTURE: Quarter to it.

PAST: Thank you quarter to.

FUTURE: We can't do this job in two days. It's not possible.

PAST: We have no choice. We must.

FUTURE: Or what? Are we all on the line here?

PAST: This punishment is due to your actions!

FUTURE: Don't even try to blame me for this. You're the reason we're under a damn microscope.

PAST: And your contriving is the reason we have just been stripped of a day's worth of time.

FUTURE: It was one cinnamon stick!

PAST: That single stick of cinnamon was a departure from the recipe. "Deviation is unacceptable." Those were the words I used to–

FUTURE: Don't you even dare. This isn't my fault.

PAST: Your insolence, your idiocy, your improvisation–

FUTURE: Hey! Only one of us has a history of improvisation hurting someone.

At FUTURE's *line,* PAST *becomes deeply serious. She draws in close to* FUTURE *in a dominant stance that he knows all too well. Even* PRESENT *is intimidated, and they don't even know what's going on.*

PAST: You have forgotten your place, ghost.

The clock chimes for the hour. The sound of its bell crashes down like a brick through glass.

FUTURE: *(to* PAST, *angry but toeing the line)* And that's the hour itself.

PAST: *(pointedly)* Thank you.

PAST *shakes off their exchange and crosses to the upstage curtain like nothing has just happened.* FUTURE *sits down.* PRESENT *is so lost.*

The clock rings out one o'clock and light begins to shine through the upstage curtain.

PRESENT: *(quietly, to* FUTURE) Are you alright?

FUTURE *does not respond.*

PAST: *(calling through the curtain)* Ebenezer... Ebenezer... Ebenezer Scrooge!

PAST *throws open the curtain upstage and a cool, but near blinding light pours out. She exits into the light and the curtain closes behind her.*

The lights fade down.

PRESENT: *(in darkness)* Whoa...

Stave II

Stave II
The Ghost of Christmas Past

As the lights slowly rise, PAST *is overheard working.* FUTURE *is on the couch, his dossier open on his lap, but he isn't reading.* PRESENT, *now in their early 20's, listens closely by the wassail, taking notes.*

SCROOGE: *(V.O.)* Are you the spirit whose coming was foretold to me?

PAST: *(V.O. or Offstage)* I am.

SCROOGE: *(V.O.)* Who, and what are you?

PAST: *(V.O. or Offstage)* I am the Ghost of Christmas Past.

SCROOGE: *(V.O.)* Long past?

PAST: *(V.O. or Offstage)* No. Your past.

SCROOGE: *(V.O.)* What business brings you here?

PAST: *(V.O. or Offstage)* Your welfare.

SCROOGE: *(V.O.)* I should think a good night's rest would–

PAST: *(V.O. or Offstage)* Your reclamation, then! Take heed!

PRESENT: Ooh... That's a good line!

> *They jot down a note.* FUTURE *lets out a huge, frustrated sigh.*

PRESENT: *(cont'd)* You alright?

FUTURE: Hmm? Oh, I'll get over it.

PRESENT: That got really intense before.

FUTURE: Yeah, Past... Well, she's always just done her own thing.

PRESENT: Do you think we can do it? Help Mister Scrooge in only two days?

FUTURE: We don't have much of a choice, do we?

PRESENT: Just like that?

FUTURE: *(more bitterly than he intends)* Live in the moment. It's what you do, right?

PRESENT: I still don't understand - are we being punished?

FUTURE: She's being punished. We're caught in the crossfire, apparently. You read 1841's file?

PRESENT: I- well- not yet, no.

FUTURE: The office didn't start you with that one? Oof. That explains a lot.

PRESENT: Could you catch me up?

FUTURE: If you're looking for the Cliff Notes version, there isn't one, and I'm not in the mood for telling sad stories.

PRESENT: Sad? How?

FUTURE: Like I said...

> PRESENT *drops the subject.*

FUTURE: *(cont'd)* She's always been a shitty communicator.

PRESENT: Hmm?

FUTURE: For as long as we've been working together - which is a long bloody time - she's been like this. Keeping things to herself. Acting like I don't need to know about things.

PRESENT: Oh.

FUTURE: It was one cinnamon stick. One. All she had to do was tell me "Hey, don't muck this up. If any of us muck up, it's not just me that's going down for it." But did she? NO! She decided to keep that little nugget of knowledge for herself and–

PRESENT: Were you going to do anything about it?

FUTURE: What's that supposed to mean?

PRESENT: Oh, well, it's just that- I've noticed that- Umm... You do everything she tells you to.

FUTURE: What? No, I don't.

PRESENT: Sure, you do. You did right before she left.

FUTURE: That's ridiculous.

PRESENT: There are examples in nearly every case file.

FUTURE: I- She- We–

PRESENT: It's always the same:

> *(mimicking* FUTURE*)*

Joke-y joke, snarky snarky, blah blah.

> *(mimicking* PAST*)*

Future.

> *(mimicking* FUTURE*)*

Right.

> *A beat.*

> FUTURE *realizes* PRESENT *is right. It's a glass shattering moment.*

FUTURE: Well, I'll be damned... *(a beat)* I need a drink.

FUTURE *begins a search of the room, checking behind books, under the sofa, etc.*

PRESENT: What are you looking for?

FUTURE: My dignity.

PRESENT: Is that really necess–

FUTURE: I'm such an idiot! Why have I let this go on for centuries??

PRESENT: I couldn't say.

FUTURE: That was obviously a rhetorical question.

PRESENT: It was?

FUTURE: You know what the worst part is?

PRESENT: Is this rhetorical or...?

FUTURE: She wasn't even supposed to be here this year!

PRESENT: She wasn't?

FUTURE: No! But she just saunters in after two years like she owns the place and expects me to bow down and obey like a little baby New Year!

PRESENT: *(under his breath)* Well, you did...

FUTURE: Where in the blazes is my Share?!

PRESENT: Your share of what?

FUTURE: My Angel's Share.

PRESENT: Come again?

FUTURE: My Angel's Share. It's the byproduct of the aging process of alcohol–a liquid intoxicant favoured by humans. It helps me forg–*(catching himself)*. Focus. It helps me focus.

PRESENT: And it's hidden because... ?

FUTURE: Because the Ghost of Forlorn Shagging - that's Valentine's Day Past to you - is a damn lush. Not that I can blame him... You gonna sit there like a dodo or you going to help me look?

PRESENT: *(indicating the wassail)* I'm trying to observe. You know, be in the moment?

FUTURE: I see what you did there...

PRESENT: Truthfully, though, I'm taking notes, studying, re-reading The Plan. I know the timeline's stressed now, but I feel alright about it!

FUTURE: Wow! That's so great!

PRESENT: Sarcasm?

FUTURE: Me? Never! Now help me find the Share.

> PRESENT *begins to protest, but is cut off.*

FUTURE: *(cont'd)* You can start over there.

> PRESENT *reluctantly, and unenthusiastically, joins the search. They try to make small talk.*

PRESENT: So... Past wasn't going to be back this year?

FUTURE: Not as far as I knew.

PRESENT: But, why?

FUTURE: Read the file.

PRESENT: You don't like talking about it.

FUTURE: I moved on.

PRESENT: Past–

FUTURE: She doesn't like talking about it either. But it's all she's thinking about, trust me. Living in the past is, you know, what she does. If you're going to try to psychoanalyze me, I'd suggest reading that file first so you know what you're talking about. Nice try, though.

> *(finding the bottle)*

Aha! There you are, my sweet essence of being.

> *(to* PRESENT*)*

Come, have a snifter with me.

PRESENT: *(realizing that* FUTURE *has moved on to shinier things)* I have some more reading to do.

FUTURE: If that's where your evening's heading, then you're definitely gonna need some of this!

> *As he speaks,* FUTURE *finds two cups and pours. The Angel's Share has an ethereal glimmer to it. He offers one to* PRESENT.

PRESENT: I don't believe that would be appropriate.

FUTURE: *(offering a cup)* Pulling an all-nighter isn't good for anyone.

PRESENT: I mean... *(he catches a whiff from the glass)* Ooh! That smells good!

FUTURE: I know, right?

PRESENT: Alright. Just one.

FUTURE: Thatta boy.

PRESENT: What could go wrong?

> FUTURE *and* PRESENT *clink their glasses and the lights drop. As it does, the sounds of* PAST's *work rise.*

PAST: *(V.O. or Offstage)* The place. Do you know it?

SCROOGE: *(V.O.)* Know it! Was I apprenticed here? *(A jolly laugh echoes.)* Why it's old Fezziwig! Bless his heart, it's Fezziwig alive again!

> *That laugh leads a chorus of sounds from Fezziwig's party echoing through - singing, dancing, laughter (especially Fezziwig's), and great amounts of merriment. At the height of Scrooge's enjoyment of this memory, a woman's giggles rise above the rest.*

SCROOGE: *(V.O.) (his voice breaking)* I know that voice. It's her, is it not? It's... Belle...

PAST: *(V.O. or Offstage)* My time grows short.

SCROOGE: *(V.O.)* No! Wait!

PAST: *(V.O. or Offstage)* Quick!

> *The sounds of the party fade, leaving Belle's gentle laughter lingering.*
>
> *The lights fade up.* FUTURE *has dozed off in a chair.* PRESENT *is fast asleep, draped ungracefully on the couch with their head resting on the open Plan.*
>
> PAST *pops her head through the upstage curtain.*

PAST: Psst! Future? Future!

> *No response from either spirit.*

PAST: *(cont'd)* Oy! The Angel's Share is gone!

FUTURE: *(popping awake)* What?? No!

PAST: Look here, you sot.

FUTURE: Past! Hey! What's up, girl?

Her glare could send a shiver down even Scrooge's back...
(well, maybe not, but you get the idea)

FUTURE: *(cont'd)* I only had the one.

PAST: Save your lies for another time and rouse Present.

FUTURE: What time is it? You can't be finished already.

PAST: Future!

FUTURE: Right. *(giving PRESENT a wake-up shove)* Get up!

PRESENT: *(still a little drunk and now in their late 20's)* Hmm? What's going on? What's happening?

PAST: Is he intoxicated?

FUTURE: No comment.

PAST: Hear me, both of you: Scrooge is weakened already.

FUTURE: What the hell did you do to him?

PAST: This is no time for your jests.

PRESENT: When you say "weakened..."

PAST: I suspect he could break at any moment.

FUTURE: Oh shit.

PRESENT: What do we do?

PAST: I have a thought. 'Tis a risk–

PRESENT: What kind of a risk?

FUTURE: If you're thinking what I think you're thinking, then absolutely not. I won't allow it.

PRESENT: Allow what?

PAST: *(to FUTURE)* Have you a stronger proposal?

FUTURE: If you gave me a damn second to–

PRESENT: Anyone care to fill me in?

FUTURE: Wouldn't this classify as a "deviation?" What's gonna happen if–

PAST: I cannot be faulted for variation if it is in the best interest of the subject–

PRESENT: Hello? What is happening??

FUTURE: Do you want to tell him, or should I? *(turning to* PRESENT *before* PAST *can speak)* She wants to speed up the timeline.

PRESENT: But we've already lost a day! That would mean–

PAST: Completing this mission in one night.

PRESENT: That's not possible!

FUTURE: Past, if Scrooge's walls have come down this much already, are you sure this is the safest option?

PAST: I do not see any alternatives before me.

FUTURE: I literally wrote another option. It was in my hands. It was beautiful...

PAST: Do you refer to your plan? Your "Super Special– "

FUTURE: "Super Awesome Plan to Save Scrooge's Soul."

PAST: Future, your plan was–

FUTURE: Brilliant? Well thought out? Unread by you?

PAST: Excessively titled and unnecessary.

FUTURE: You cocky banshee.

PRESENT: Hey! There's no need for language like that!

PAST: Insolence does not suit your character.

FUTURE: A man's soul is on the line, Past!

PAST: Aye! And Scrooge weakens sooner than anticipated - did you foresee such a development? Does your "plan" account for such a possibility?

FUTURE: We've already lost a day on a case that needed a full three days. What's the office gonna do to us if you do this?

PAST: The administration be damned. They may believe he requires such time, but *(she points to herself)* we do not. I have assessed the situation and believe this to be the proper course of action. Do you not believe me? Look upon him and see for yourself how his lip trembles.

> FUTURE *crosses to the wassail and looks in. She's right and he knows it - but he'll be damned if he admits it out loud right now.*

PAST: *(cont'd)* I was correct, was I not?

> FUTURE *cedes his ground.* PRESENT *takes note of this, but doesn't say anything.*

FUTURE: How much time does Present have?

PRESENT: But, the Plan–

PAST: Another shadow, perhaps two, to take Scrooge through, but it will not take long. Scrooge's walls are coming down, hastily.

PRESENT: I'm getting lost in all this jargon. What does that mean? Weakening, breaking, walls...?

FUTURE: The walls are a metaphor for the state of his... psyche.

PAST: For us to lead him to salvation, 'tis insufficient for Scrooge to feel remorse and beg forgiveness. He must make a commitment to change and redemption, otherwise our work is for naught.

FUTURE: But if we push him too hard, we run the risk of losing him to regret and sorrow. If the truth overwhelms him, his mind will break and–*(shooting a glance over to* PAST*)*– There's no coming back from that.

PAST: If he breaks, we fail. Failure is not an option. Time and Fate are watching. *(to* FUTURE*)* Proceed.

PRESENT: Hold on. Are we not going to talk about this? Together? As a team?

PAST: *(to* FUTURE*, with no acknowledgement of* PRESENT*)* Do. it.

PRESENT: Is this really happening??

> FUTURE *takes a ladle and stirs the wassail clockwise in two wide circles.*
>
> *The clock strikes.*

FUTURE: That's a quarter past, Present.

PRESENT: Sweet merciful Fate!

FUTURE: That she ain't.

PAST: I know from experience.

> *From the wassail bowl,* SCROOGE'S *voice emanates.*

SCROOGE: *(V.O.)* Spirit! Show me no more!

PAST: I must return.

> PAST *crosses to the curtain.*

PAST: *(cont'd) (to* FUTURE*, pointing to* PRESENT*)* Get them up to speed.

SCROOGE: *(V.O.)* Conduct me home! Why do you delight to torture me?

> PAST *exits behind the curtain.*

PAST: *(Offstage)* One shadow more!

> PRESENT *starts to panic.*

PRESENT: What are we going to do?

FUTURE: Well, I'm going to have some more Share. You better start rereading The Plan.

PRESENT: Like that's any good anymore!

FUTURE: *(pouring himself some Angel's Share)* What're you talking about?

> *The clock chimes.*

FUTURE: *(cont'd)* That's half past.

PRESENT: What am I gonna do? If Scrooge is "breaking" as you say, then the Plan is useless!

FUTURE: You need to pull yourself together.

PRESENT: What does it matter? I'm not prepared for this and Scrooge is doomed and I'll never amount to anything.

FUTURE: Oh wow.

PRESENT: Time is so short.

FUTURE: Hey! Listen to me.

> PRESENT *reluctantly does so.*

FUTURE: *(cont'd)* Your time here is short. And the time you've been given is intended to help redeem one man's soul and save him from eternal damnation. Do you want to mope around, do nothing, and damn Scrooge? Do you?

PRESENT: No, but... What do I do? Improvise??

FUTURE: Well, we certainly don't want that. What was it that The Plan wants you to do?

PRESENT: Show him the workhouses and factories; the workers there and the sick and the poor on the streets.

FUTURE: Ugh. How depressing.

PRESENT: How is any of that supposed to inspire any sort of change in Scrooge?

FUTURE: Great question...

PRESENT: You see why I'm worried?

> *The clock chimes again.*

FUTURE: *(cont'd)* Quarter to.

PRESENT: *(collapsing onto the couch)* Don't remind me.

FUTURE: *(an idea striking)* Well, I'll be a monkey's uncle!

> *He swiftly grabs his binder and hands it to* PRESENT.

PRESENT: Your plan?

FUTURE: You remember my ideas for you?

PRESENT: Yes, but–

FUTURE: Call it a back-up plan–and you're going to use it!

PRESENT: I don't know...

FUTURE: *(flipping to a page)* Scrooge lives in a world of suffering, and has the power to change not only his life, but the lives of many.

PRESENT: But in a world–in an era–as bleak as this, is there hope for him? For Scrooge?

FUTURE: There is hope if we lead him to it - if you lead him to it. Your role is vital to his survival. Vital.

PRESENT: What happens to him if we fail?

FUTURE: I don't know...

PRESENT: Why am I so hungry right now?

FUTURE: Use it.

PRESENT: Use what?

FUTURE: The hunger you feel–it's empathy. Let it fuel you. Show Scrooge what he chooses to ignore. Make him feel as you do–as the people do.

PRESENT: Yes! Of course! Why didn't I think of that?

> *The clock chimes again.*

FUTURE: The hour itself. You can do this.

PRESENT: I can do this!

FUTURE: *(looking* PRESENT *over)* But not in that outfit.

PRESENT: What's wrong with what I'm wearing?

FUTURE: Bland, bland, bland. We need to Christmas you up...

> (FUTURE *looks around and finally checks out the robe he's wearing. He removes it hastily, turning it inside out to reveal a velvety green lining.)*

Here. Throw this on.

PRESENT: *(putting the robe on)* How do I look?

FUTURE: Hmm. Not quite there yet.

FUTURE *looks about the room, then reaches into* PAST's *dressing room and finds a white stole. He drapes it over* PRESENT's *shoulders. The look is closer, but not quite right. Looking around again, he spots a ring of holly on a table. He sets it on* PRESENT's *head and the image is complete. For the audience, it is a very familiar look.*

FUTURE: *(cont'd)* There we are. You're ready now!

PRESENT *takes their place at the curtain. They take a deep breath and look back to* FUTURE.

FUTURE: Give him hell.

PRESENT *nods. The curtain opens to reveal a chaise lounge covered in foods of all kinds, bathed in warm firelight. Ecstatic at the sight of food,* PRESENT's *booming, delighted laughter carries them through the curtain. As they cross the threshold into the light, the curtain closes behind them and the lights go down.*

Stave III

Stave III
The Ghost of Christmas Present

As the lights rise, PRESENT *is overheard working.* FUTURE
sits on the couch. PAST *watches the wassail intently. They
are decidedly not speaking to one another.*

PRESENT: Come in! Come in and know me better, man!

SCROOGE: *(V.O.)* You are–

PRESENT: I am the Ghost of Christmas Present! Look upon
me. You have never seen the like of me before!

SCROOGE: *(V.O.)* Spirit, conduct me where you will. I went
forth last night on compulsion, and I learnt
a lesson that is working now. Tonight, if you
have aught to teach me, let me profit by it.

PRESENT: Touch my robe!

PAST: "Touch my robe?" What sort of line is that?

FUTURE: A good one. *(A beat)* Are we talking now?

PAST: Future.

FUTURE: Right. Shut up. Cool. Cool cool cool.

> *Another beat.*

PAST: *(looking closer)* Are they wearing...?

FUTURE: My robe? Yeah. Yeah, they are.

PAST: They look a half-naked fool.

FUTURE: What're you talking about? They're working that robe!

PAST: They work nothing.

> *Another beat.* FUTURE *wants to talk, but doesn't push it.*

PAST: Are they taking Scrooge for a bloody walk?

FUTURE: What do you mean? Where are they?

PAST: Nowhere.

FUTURE: Could you be a little more specific?

PAST: The city streets.

FUTURE: Oh, interesting take.

PAST: What "take" would that be?

FUTURE: An empathetic one.

PAST: They are demonstrating empathy by taking a bloody walk? What good is intended there?

FUTURE: They're showing Scrooge the warmth of humanity.

PAST: Scrooge is a misanthrope. Those people hold no meaning for him.

FUTURE: Give them a chance, Past.

PAST: Bestow a chance to whom? Our charge, or Present?

FUTURE: They were floundering. The Plan for their visit was too bleak. They needed the push.

PAST: You coached them.

FUTURE: You told me to get them up to speed.

PAST: Bring them to speed—not give them alms as though they were a beggar! Year after year you nurse them like infants. You do more preparation for Present than you do for yourself!

FUTURE: What makes you think I'm not prepared?

PAST: You are not yet properly clothed.

FUTURE: At least I give them some sort of guidance, instead of regarding them with indifference and condescension!

PAST: "Guidance?" Is that what you are calling it this year?

FUTURE: We put in all this work so that Present can use their instincts, use the time—what little of it they have—and the environment to influence the subject to, in their hearts, find—

PAST: That is not the function of this position! They cannot work on "heart" alone!

FUTURE: And why not?

PAST: They are too young.

FUTURE: They age too fast to ever be "too young." Why must everything be so black and white with you?

PAST: For humans, it is! There is life and there is death. How can it be anymore black and white than that?

FUTURE: So you speed up the timeline and risk everything? What are you trying to prove, Past?

PAST: Those in the office, they are trying to push me out. They want me gone.

FUTURE: If you had just accepted responsibility—

PAST: If you are attempting to segue into a discussion of 1841, naught but disappointment awaits you.

FUTURE: I've gotten used to that.

PAST: What is your intention with such a statement?

FUTURE: You've lost all sense of care you once had.

PAST: You accuse me of indifference? As opposed to your sloth-fulness? Is this what the world comes to? Insouciance and laziness?

FUTURE: For centuries, you've refused to give me any responsi-bility or say around here and then you call me lazy? Cool. Awesome. Great.

PAST: I would have bestowed you with some responsibility if you had, even once, shown some semblance of effort.

FUTURE: How does this keep coming back to me being lazy?

PAST: If this indignant behavior stems from the disregard your plan received, then come out and say it.

FUTURE: You are insufferable.

PAST: Do you wish to end the conversation, Future? Then simply indicate as such. I have had quite enough insults for one year.

FUTURE: I don't–Ugh. Nevermind.

> *Laughter from the Cratchit household emanates from the wassail.* FUTURE *crosses to investigate.*

FUTURE: Huh. *(to* PAST*)* Come look at this.

PAST: Wherefore?

> FUTURE *throws her an annoyed look.* PAST *begrudgingly crosses to the wassail but doesn't look in.*

PAST: *(cont'd)* What am I to glean from this?

FUTURE: The places where, despite the bleak darkness of their world, hope and light shine through.

PAST: From where does this eloquence stem? Do you remain inebriated?

FUTURE: You are so obnoxious. Look where Present has taken Scrooge.

PAST: *(looking into the wassail)* The Cratchit house?

FUTURE: It's a good call on their part.

PAST: To what end? Seeing their life will only prove Scrooge's point, making this wasted time.

FUTURE: Yeah, the Cratchits' lives are hard and they don't have a lot of comforts, but look at the joy and love in that house. And the ribbons! So many ribbons...

PAST: How is this relevant?

SCROOGE: *(V.O.)* Spirit, tell me if Tiny Tim will live.

PRESENT: *(V.O. or Offstage)* I see a vacant seat in the poor chimney-corner, and a crutch without an owner, carefully preserved. If these shadows remain unaltered by the Future, the child will die.

SCROOGE: *(V.O.)* No, no! Oh no, kind Spirit, say he will be spared!

PRESENT: *(V.O. or Offstage)* If these shadows remain unaltered by the Future, none other of my race will find him here. What then? If he be like to die, he had better do it, and decrease the surplus population.

FUTURE: Oh damn. They went there.

PAST: Using Scrooge's own words against him... An inspired choice.

FUTURE: Just because they used something from your Plan–

47

PAST: The Plan.

FUTURE: –doesn't make it "inspired."

PRESENT: *(V.O. or Offstage)* Man, if man you be in heart, forbear that wicked cant until you have discovered What the surplus is, and Where it is. Will you decide what men shall live, what men shall die? It may be, that in the sight of Heaven, you are more worthless and less fit to live than millions like this poor man's child.

PAST: *(more to herself than anyone else)* The child...?

FUTURE: Scrooge found a hint of light that he doesn't want extinguished. First time in a long time.

PAST: He has opened his bed curtains only a sliver, but what will he do about what he sees? If Present–

FUTURE: Present is making Scrooge face the truths that he has been hiding from, that he shut out to protect himself. Isn't that what we want?

PAST: Not if Present touches on something from which Scrooge will be unable return.

FUTURE: On that subject–

PAST: Future–

FUTURE: We need to stop sidestepping the issue here. Your last case is–no pun intended–haunting us.

PAST: What more is there to say? The administration's thoughts on the matter were made abundantly clear. Time and Fate–

FUTURE: Past, stop making yourself out to be the victim.

PAST: Is that what you think?

FUTURE: Yes! And you need to get over it.

PAST: I cannot.

> *A beat. This should be the first real moment of silence since they started talking.*

> FUTURE *is unsure of how to respond to her honesty.*

PAST: *(cont'd)* I cannot "get over it," as you so desire. As you do, so easily. My entire existence revolves around the past, the things that have already been, around lessons hard learned and lost. I live in it always, and always I must watch you move forward, unable to do so myself. 'Get over it?' You speak as though you understand me, but you know nothing of my struggles.

FUTURE: I do, though.

> *(raising his glass of Angel's Share)*

What do you think this is for?

PAST: You are lucky to have a method of coping. 'Tis more than I have.

> FUTURE *sets the glass down and pushes it away.*

PAST: *(cont'd)* You want to speak of my last case? You want to discuss that poor man—the case we thought 'simple'? We had no way of knowing how much he would resist.

FUTURE: But he did, and we let hubris guide our actions. '41 and I, we...

> *He hesitates before continuing, knowing the implications of what he's about to say out loud*

We followed you blindly—

PAST: You mean to place the blame entirely on my shoulders?!

FUTURE: *(done toeing the line)* You made the call to to speed up the timeline! That was your decision—you never even paused to consult us, to consider our subject. You rushed us and pushed too hard.

PAST: *(struggling to find a defense)* We needed a redemptive commitment from him. I could not have known...

FUTURE: Say it. We pushed him to it. I want to hear you say it.

PAST: *(a beat of hesitation before she continues)* We- I did not think he would... take his own life.

FUTURE: And there it is.

> A beat as FUTURE *tries to process his anger.*

PAST: *(a little quietly)* I thought you would have warned me. I thought... you would have looked–

FUTURE: You know that's not how it works.

PAST: I only thought–

FUTURE: You only thought of yourself. As always.

> PAST *has no rebuttal.*

FUTURE: *(cont'd)* That poor soul is going to wander the world for eternity, unable to atone for his sins, because of what you did and tonight? Tonight you decide to do it again? Whose soul are you trying to save—Scrooge's? Or your own?

> A long beat. PAST *is unsure of how to continue.*

PAST: I am–

FUTURE: Try to apologize when you mean it. In the meantime, take a good hard look at yourself: if you feel nothing–no guilt, no sadness, no regret–then perhaps it is time for you to–to move on.

The clock chimes. Its timing is unfortunate, but both spirits lay down their proverbial arms and return to a business decorum.

PAST: Quarter past.

FUTURE: Back to business. *(sitting down)* Thank you quarter past.

PAST: You sit? Have you no preparations to make?

FUTURE: Oh, I'm prepared.

PAST: I cannot discern if you are in earnest or jest.

FUTURE: Isn't this fun?

PAST: Future.

FUTURE: Past.

PAST: Right...

FUTURE: Don't you want to be surprised?

PAST: I detest surprises.

FUTURE: I'll give you a hint: Gonna go with a classic this year.

The clock chimes again.

PAST: Half past.

FUTURE: Thank you half past.

PAST: Have it all figured out, do you? This case, our subject?

FUTURE: No, not in the least. You're just seeing Scrooge as an irreparable old painting that needs to come down. I'm seeing what remains of his paint.

A beat.

PAST: What an awful metaphor.

FUTURE: Yeah, I could hear it while I was saying it, but it was too late to stop myself.

PAST: You should work on that. Read more Shakespeare.

FUTURE: It's been a while. I've been really into graphic novels this year.

PAST: "Graphic novels?"

FUTURE: They're books made up of cartoons. Illustrations, really.

PAST: You spent a year reading children's books?

FUTURE: No. Well, occasionally. Mostly for adults, though.

PAST: You may borrow the first Folio. A little Shakespeare ought to do you some good.

FUTURE: You're not wrong there.

The clock chimes again.

PAST: Quarter to.

FUTURE: Thank you quarter to.

> PAST *crosses to the wassail and watches as* PRESENT*'s work comes to an end.* FUTURE *crosses to his dressing room door.*

PAST: They have aged so swiftly.

FUTURE: *(reaching into his dressing room and pulling out a pair of boots, which he puts on as he listens)* Well, Scrooge's having a hell of a night.

PAST: No, Present...

FUTURE: How're they bringing it home?

PAST: It appears as though they are utilizing the Vices... as children...

FUTURE: The sister, the boy, the vices–kids is a good throughline.

SCROOGE: *(V.O.)* Are spirits' lives so short?

PRESENT: *(V.O. or Offstage)* My life upon this globe, is very brief. It ends tonight.

SCROOGE: *(V.O.)* Tonight!

PRESENT: *(V.O. or Offstage)* Tonight at midnight. Hark! The time is drawing near.

SCROOGE: *(V.O.)* Spirit, forgive me if I am not justified in what I ask, but I see something strange, and not belonging to yourself, protruding from your skirts. Is it a foot or a claw?

PRESENT: *(V.O. or Offstage)* It might be a claw, for the flesh there is upon it. Look here.

FUTURE: Not pullin' any punches, are they?

PAST: On the subject of not pulling punches, when you say you intend to "go with a classic" do you mean to–

> *A mischievous smile grows on* FUTURE'S *face as he pops into his dressing room.*

PAST: *(cont'd)* You have not dusted that one off since- How long has it been?

FUTURE: *(Offstage)* Couple centuries, I think? Blink of an eye, really.

PRESENT: *(V.O. or Offstage)* Oh, Man! look here. Look, look, down here!

SCROOGE: *(V.O.)* Spirit! Are they yours?

PRESENT: *(V.O. or Offstage)* They are Man's, and they cling to me, appealing from their fathers. This boy is Ignorance. This girl is Want. Beware them both, and all of their degree, but most of all beware this boy, for on his brow I see that written which is Doom, unless the writing be erased.

SCROOGE: *(V.O.)* Have they no refuge or resource?

PRESENT: *(V.O. or Offstage)* Are there no prisons? Are there no workhouses?

PAST: *(turning back to observe the wassail; to* FUTURE*)* Striking the fear of God into Scrooge is a good move. Strong ending.

FUTURE: *(Offstage)* Oh, I'm not striking the fear of God into him.

PAST: What then? What could you do that would frighten him more?

FUTURE: *(entering)* I'm striking him with the fear of Time.

> *The lights flicker and there is a clap of thunder and lightning. When the lights correct themselves,* FUTURE *stands in the green room as the embodiment of all Ghosts of Christmas Future we know: clad grimly in dark robes with his face obscured. When he moves, it appears as though he is gliding rather than walking.*

PAST: Finish it.

> FUTURE *nods his reply. The upstage curtain opens and fog rolls in. The light on the other side is dim and ominous. The curtain closes after* FUTURE *crosses the threshold. Lights go down.*

Stave IV

Stave IV
The Ghost of Christmas Yet to Come

As the lights rise, we hear SCROOGE *speaking to* FUTURE. PRESENT, *now in their 40-50's with salt and pepper hair, watches the wassail intently.* PAST *paces quietly in the back, buried in her thoughts.*

SCROOGE: *(V.O.)* I am in the presence of the Ghost of Christmas Yet To Come?

There is no reply.

SCROOGE: *(V.O.)* You are about to show me shadows of the things that have not happened, but will happen in the time before us. Is that so, Spirit?

PRESENT: He's trembling. Mister Scrooge is trembling.

PAST: *(with no desire to engage)* Hmm.

SCROOGE: *(V.O.)* Ghost of the Future! I fear you more than any spectre I have seen. But as I know your purpose is to do me good, and as I hope to live to be another man from what I was, I am prepared to bear you company, and do it with a thankful heart. Will you not speak to me?

SCROOGE *receives no reply.*

SCROOGE: *(V.O.)* Lead on! Lead on! The night is waning fast, and it is precious time to me, I know. Lead on, Spirit!

PRESENT: What is Future doing? Why isn't he speaking? *(thinking* PAST *can't hear them)* Past? Hello?

PAST: I believe he calls it "ghosting."

PRESENT: Isn't that what we've been doing all night?

PAST: One would think as much, but no, the term is reappropri-
ated in the future. Something to do with an utter cease in
communication, or some such nonsense.

PRESENT: That seems really inconsiderate.

PAST: I, myself, understand very little of the future world, but
this certainly is... a choice.

PRESENT: How do you mean?

PAST: By not speaking, he leads Scrooge to draw his own con-
clusions, forcing him to find his own way to redemption.
If he must find it himself, he stands a higher chance of
commitment.

PRESENT: Future's taking a very dark approach...

PAST: "Impossible" jobs call for more... creative modi operandi.

PRESENT: But couldn't this push Mister Scrooge too far? The
darkness, the fog, the cemetery... the imagery alone is–

PAST: We have not yet come to a close.

> *A beat.*

PRESENT: Any predictions? For how this will all turn out?

PAST: At this juncture, I cannot say...

PRESENT: It's gone well so far. Would you agree? I expected a
much bigger fight, to be honest. More resistance. The
Plan was clearly formulated with a similar expectation.
Are you surprised by the evening's turn of events?

PAST: How this line of questioning pertinent?

PRESENT: Is everything alright? Are you alright?

PAST: Wherefore would I not be?

PRESENT: You seem... different, somehow. Somber.

PAST: What stake do you hold in my well being?

PRESENT: An emotional one? Did something happen while I was visiting Scrooge? Was it Future? Did he say someth–

PAST: You make a great deal of assumptions, wisp. You would do well to cease such thoughts.

PRESENT: *(tickled by her grumpiness; trying to maintain a light tone)* Why are you being so prickly? The job is going well, expediting the timeline seems to have been the correct choice, Mister Scrooge has made some break-throughs, and you're acting like it could go sideways at any moment!

PAST: After centuries in this line of work, I am overly cognizant of the fact that, with the job not yet completed, anything is possible. We do not know what Scrooge could do. The slightest action - a word, a motion, a breath - can affect the entire operation.

PRESENT: Alright, but our "deviation" from the Plan seems to not have had a negative impact?

PAST: Aye, I am certain that your... "creativity" will be taken into account.

PRESENT: I don't see our "creativity" in a negative way.

PAST: No? And what is it that you do see?

PRESENT: To be honest? It has nothing to do with Mister Scrooge.

PAST: Oh?

PRESENT: Your struggle to maintain control of this department is glaringly obvious.

PAST: I beg your pardon?

PRESENT: I think you feel like you've lost your grip on this place and that terrifies you.

> *And without even trying,* PRESENT *has shattered the glass for* PAST. *They're having a hard time reading her expression.*

PRESENT: *(cont'd)* Uh... Are you alright?

PAST: Perhaps the administration is correct. Perhaps it is time for me to retire.

PRESENT: You can't do that!

PAST: What other options are before me?

PRESENT: Working! Saving souls! Mentoring young Spirits for years to come!

PAST: Is not that all tainted?

PRESENT: What are you talking about? Of course not! I idolized you when I was a younger spirit. I still do!

PAST: I cannot fathom your view of me. Do you remain ignorant of ou–*(this is hard for her to say)* my actions on my last case?

PRESENT: Future alluded to it, but I never got to finish reading the file.

PAST: Then your optimism is unfounded.

PRESENT: It's eating away at you.

PAST: Optimism? Highly unlikely.

PRESENT: No, your last subject.

PAST: Do not assume that you know–

PRESENT: Past, you know you can't move on with unfinished business, right?

A beat.

PAST: Future was correct–you certainly do not "pull your punches," do you?

PRESENT: Aren't we all too old for that now?

A pause. PAST *takes a seat.*

PAST: I cannot cease thinking of him.

PRESENT: He died, didn't he?

PAST: *(quietly)* He–He took his–

She can't continue. PRESENT *places a reassuring hand on her shoulder.*

PRESENT: I'm sorry. I'm sorry that happened.

PAST: All this time, I have roamed these halls with him always in my thoughts. I have laboured at that desk turning the events of that night over and over in my mind. It has been two years, yet it feels a lifetime.

PRESENT: That must have been very hard for you to carry.

PAST: I remain unable to shake my... my guilt.

PRESENT: So this year you wanted to make it right.

PAST: For my benefit only, perhaps. For my own selfish purposes.

PRESENT: There is a way to move forward, you know. Not just move on. One defeat doesn't need to define you.

PAST: You speak as though it were a simple gesture. I am not a Ghost of the Future. I cannot glide through existence with no thought of history.

PRESENT: Maybe you can learn something from him.

PAST: You are humorous.

PRESENT: Do you realize that the two of you need what the other can't give? He needs you to accept what's happened and move forward, you need him to reflect and learn from your history. There must be some middle ground there.

PAST: We have been working alongside one another for too long, I fear, for us to find a middle ground.

PRESENT: Then try not to dwell on those you could not help. Think instead of those you've saved. Those people whose lives you've altered for the better. How many are there? Hundreds? Focus on them. Remember them. Remember the change you led them to make.

PAST: It is not so simple.

PRESENT: It could be, if you let it.

SCROOGE: *(V.O.)* Am I that man that lay upon the bed?

PAST: This is it.

> *They cross to wassail to observe.*

SCROOGE: *(V.O.)* No, Spirit! Oh no, no! Spirit! Hear me! I am not the man I was. I will not be the man I must have been but for this intercourse. Why show me this, if I am past all hope?

> *The spirits take a deep breath - will this go the way they hope?*

SCROOGE: *(V.O.)* Good Spirit, your nature intercedes for me, and pities me. Assure me that I yet may change these shadows you have shown me, by an altered life!

PAST grasps PRESENT's hand - neither can believe what they've just heard.

SCROOGE: *(V.O.)* I will honour Christmas in my heart, and try to keep it all the year. I will live in the Past, the Present, and the Future. The Spirits of all Three shall strive within me. I will not shut out the lessons that they teach. Oh, tell me I may sponge away the writing on this stone!

Upon hearing this, PAST and PRESENT let out a celebratory cheer.

PAST & PRESENT: We did it!

PRESENT throws their arms around PAST in an excited embrace, unaware of her being overcome with emotion. She sniffles and wipes something away from her eye...

PRESENT: Are you–Is that–

PAST: Speak nothing of this to Future.

PRESENT: My lips are sealed.

PAST gathers herself and regains her composure.

PAST: *(offering her hand)* Job well done.

PRESENT: *(accepting the handshake)* Roaring success, I'd say!

PAST: Indeed.

PRESENT: You are allowed to celebrate, Past. And next year– because there will certainly be a next year–let Future lighten your load. He wants to. You don't have to do it all by yourself.

PAST: I–I shall try.

PRESENT: That's a start! *(yawning)* I could use a nap. How about you?

> PRESENT *yawns some more as they exit to their dressing room.* PAST *rolls her eyes at this as the lights fade down.*

Stave V

Stave V
The End of It

Their work completed successfully, the team can relax. PAST sips some tea as she listens to joyous sounds emit from the wassail. A weight has been lifted from her shoulders and... is that the hint of a smile? Couldn't be!

SCROOGE: *(V.O.)* I will live in the Past, the Present, and the Future! The Spirits of all Three shall strive within me. Oh Jacob Marley! Heaven, and the Christmas Time be praised for this! I say it on my knees, old Jacob; on my knees!

PAST: *(toasting Scrooge)* And a Merry Christmas to you, Ebenezer.

FUTURE: *(Offstage)* Hey! No getting started without me!

> PRESENT, *now in their 60's or 70's with grey hair, glasses, and a cane, enters from their dressing room.*

PRESENT: What was that? Are we starting?

PAST: Not yet. I was only wishing Ebenezer a "Merry Christmas."

PRESENT: Aww, that's nice... I don't think he can hear you, though.

PAST: I had a desire to say it.

FUTURE: You're talking to a bowl.

PAST: Yes, I understand.

PRESENT: *(chuckling)* You're a loon! *(A beat)* Would you like a peppermint stick?

PAST: *(genuinely)* I would love one.

PRESENT: I've got some in my pockets here...

PRESENT *searches their robe for candies. Still wearing his dark robe,* FUTURE *enters from his dressing room to join them.*

FUTURE: Well, I'd call that one a roaring success!

PAST: Yes, that is what Present said...

FUTURE: Yeah, well, I taught them everything they know. Ain't that right, old timer?

PRESENT: I'm hungry!

PAST: I must agree with you, Future. This has been a–

FUTURE: Hold on. Agreeing with me? Are you sick? Is this a trick? Am I on Candid Camera?!

PAST: Future.

FUTURE: Oh c'mon - cameras totally exist!

PAST: Motion picture cameras are some fifty years away.

FUTURE: Dammit!

PRESENT: Are you two going to banter all night?

FUTURE: I'm just reveling in this oxymoronic new Past. I'm boggled by the contradictions!

PAST: You did well this evening, Future. Very well.

FUTURE *leans forward and sniffs her.*

FUTURE: You drunk?

PAST: Take the compliment or I shall retract it.

FUTURE: *(genuinely)* Thank you.

PAST: Was that so hard?

FUTURE: I'm just having trouble processing this uncharacteristically positive attitude.

PAST: You are not alone.

FUTURE: It suits you.

PAST: As does success! This so-deemed "Impossible– "

FUTURE: Our Mission: Impossible, if you will?

PAST: I will not.

FUTURE: Okay.

PAST: We proved it quite possible, did we not? The administration–

FUTURE: Don't start that again!

PRESENT: Get on with it. I haven't got all night.

FUTURE: Shall we?

PAST: Aye.

> FUTURE *grabs three glasses, passing one each to* PAST *and* PRESENT. *They cross to the wassail.*

SCROOGE: *(V.O.)* I don't know what to do! I am as light as a feather, I am as happy as an angel, I am as merry as a schoolboy. I am as giddy as a drunken man. A merry Christmas to every-body! A happy New Year to all the world! Hallo here! Whoop! Hallo!

> FUTURE *takes the ladle and fills all three cups. They raise their cups toward the bowl.*

FUTURE: To Scrooge, and his future.

PAST & PRESENT: To Scrooge!

> *They clink their glasses and take a drink.*

PRESENT: I don't know about you two, but I've always wondered what this tasted like.

PAST: What do you think?

PRESENT: Delicious! But it needs a little extra kick, don't you think?

FUTURE: I have just the thing.

> FUTURE *reaches into his robe and produces a flask.* PAST *is not amused as he pours a little of its contents into* PRESENT'*s cup.*

PRESENT: I was thinking of cinnamon, but this will do just fine!

PAST: You took that with you into the field?

FUTURE: For emergencies, you know.

PRESENT: Ooh! Now this is tasty. Past, you should try some.

PAST: I am not much of a drinker.

FUTURE: C'mon. The job's done.

PAST: Oh, alright!

FUTURE: Atta girl.

> FUTURE *pours some of the flask's contents into her glass and his own.*

PAST: *(raising her glass)* To a roaring success!

PRESENT: I'll drink to that!

> *They clink their glasses and drink.*

PAST: Oh my. That is delectable!

FUTURE: Right?!

PRESENT: I'm gonna need to have a little sit down!

FUTURE: Need some help?

PRESENT: I'm not that old.

> PRESENT *sits down on the couch, leaving* PAST *and* FUTURE *standing by the wassail.*

FUTURE: What's brought about this shiny new attitude?

PAST: My reflections on the past have, for some time, focused solely on my own losses. Present helped me come to see that I need not do that any longer.

FUTURE: Did he now?

PAST: I do not appreciate your smug expression.

FUTURE: What smug expression?

PAST: I am attempting an earnest confession.

PRESENT: Let her talk, you poop!

FUTURE: I'm sorry.

PAST: No, Future, I am the apologetic one. I am sorry. For it all –my words, my actions–

FUTURE: Thank you.

> *They share a brief moment of reconcile.*

PAST: Perhaps next year, should I be allowed to return to my post in an official manner, we might build a Grand Plan together.

FUTURE: Do you mean it?

PAST: I do.

FUTURE: Can I name it?

PAST: Absolutely not.

FUTURE: A subtitle?

PAST: I shall take it into consideration.

FUTURE: Good enough!

PRESENT: Now shake hands or hug or something.

> *They briefly consider a hug, but* PAST *extends her hand to ease the awkwardness.* FUTURE *shakes it.*

FUTURE: This new outlook'll be good for you... Oh! New nickname! The Ghost of Reluctant Optimism!

PAST: Father Time save me...

> *An envelope slides in from under the hallway door.*

PRESENT: You hear something??

FUTURE: What's that?

PRESENT: Something from Saint Nicholas? Now he's a character!

> PAST *picks up the envelope. It is sealed with red wax and the letters "T" and "F" are embossed on the back. The front reads "The Ghost of Christmas Past."*

PAST: 'Twas sent by Father Time and Fate. Addressed to me.

> PAST *hesitates.*

PRESENT: Don't keep us waiting! Get on with it.

> PAST *nervously opens the envelope. Inside she finds a Christmas card. As she reads it,* FUTURE *and* PRESENT *lean in expectantly, trying to read* PAST's *expression. She finishes reading and closes the card.*

FUTURE: So? What's the word?

PAST: I–They–

PRESENT: Well?

PAST: Time and Fate observed our work tonight and in spite of our improvisation and deviations, they have deemed it, against all odds, our strongest success to date! They are granting my return to the field!

FUTURE: No retirement?

PAST: None!

FUTURE: Well, then, welcome home!

PRESENT: *(raising his glass)* To Past!

PAST: *(raising her glass)* To all of us.

> *They clink their glasses and take a sip.*

> *The clock chimes.*

PRESENT: That would be for me.

PAST: So soon?

> FUTURE *helps* PRESENT *up.*

PRESENT: It's bedtime, wisp.

PAST: You cannot remain a little while longer?

FUTURE: It's time, Past.

> FUTURE *extends a handshake, which* PRESENT *accepts.* PAST *embraces* PRESENT, *who is surprised by the gesture.*

PAST: Thank you.

PRESENT: What's all the fuss about?

PAST: Please, pardon my display...

PRESENT: No need for sadness. I'm part of your history now, you hear? *(to* PAST*)* Don't you go forgetting what we said.

PAST: I shall not.

PRESENT: *(to* FUTURE*)* And don't you go sailing along as if time doesn't matter.

FUTURE: I promise.

PRESENT: *(touching each of them on their forehead)* Right here, that's where I'll be.

FUTURE: Good night, Present.

PAST: Aye, good night.

PRESENT: All right, now. Be good, you two.

FUTURE: No guarantees.

PAST: I shall keep my eye on him.

PRESENT: Good night. Don't stay up too late.

PAST & FUTURE: Good night.

> PRESENT *crosses to the upstage curtain. It opens and bathes them in a warm, dreamy light. They turn around and wave.* PAST *and* FUTURE *wave back.* PRESENT *exits.*
>
> *A beat.*

FUTURE: Dang. I should've gotten my robe back...

PAST: Oh, Future!

FUTURE: It looked better on them anyway. You wanna get started on the paperwork?

PAST: Let us leave it for tomorrow.

FUTURE: I knew you'd say that.

PAST: Of course you did...

They clink glasses as the lights fade to black.

END OF PLAY

Readings

The Department of Soul Reclamation has been performed for two staged readings during its development process. It is currently looking for a home for its premier performance.

Readings:

Pocket Theater, 2017 - directed by Kathryn Stewart

ACT Theatre, 2018 - directed by Kathryn Stewart

Courtney Kessler-Jeffrey is a playwright, dresser, and producer. As a writer, her plays have been produced by Taproot Theatre (*I'll Be Home for Christmas, Cyber Zoo: It's Nothing Personal*, and a new adaptation of O. Henry's *The Gift of the Magi*), Theater Schmeater (*Welcome to My Secret Lair*), and San Juan Community Theatre (*The Dressmaker, Dear Marie Johnston, The Diagnosis*). Her latest play, *The Department of Soul Reclamation*, has been presented as a staged reading in 2017 and 2018.

As a producer, she created and ran the Seattle Play Series, a hyper-local playwriting festival, from 2013-2016 and produced *Don't Split the Party* for Transparent Storytelling Theatre in 2018. Currently, she is the Lead Dresser at ACT Theatre and has dressed at the Oregon Shakespeare Festival, Seattle Children's Theatre, Taproot Theatre Co, Seattle Shakespeare Co, Book-It Repertory, and more. She splits her time between Seattle and Friday Harbor, WA.

Made in the USA
San Bernardino, CA
14 January 2020